Ornamentation

A Question & Answer Manual

VALERY LLOYD-WATTS • CAROLE L. BIGLER

with the assistance of Willard A. Palmer

Alfred Publishing Co., Inc.
16380 Roscoe Boulevard, Suite 200
Van Nuys, California 91406

Library of Congress Cataloging-in-Publication Data
Lloyd-Watts, Valery.
    Ornamentation : a question & answer manual / by Valery Lloyd-Watts and Carole L. Bigler with the assistance of Willard A. Palmer.
        p.   cm.
    Includes bibliographical references (p.).
    ISBN 0-88284-549-7
    1. Embellishment (Music) I. Bigler, Carole L. II. Palmer, Willard A. III. Title.
    MT80.L6 1995
    781.2'47—dc20   94–13951
                                              CIP
                                              MN

Cover photograph: Große Silbermannorgel *(Great Silbermann Organ)*
                             Freiberg (Sachsen) Cathedral
                             1710–14 by Gottfried Silbermann
                             3 manual, 45 register organ
                             AKG London

Music engraving: Greg Plumblee, Linda Lusk
Book production: Kim O'Reilly, Tom Gerou
Cover art and book design: Sue Hartman

Contents

Chapter 1
Answering Your
Questions about
Ornamentation

Chapter 2
An Overview of
the Influence of Art
and Architecture on
the Development
of Music

Chapter 3
Ornamentation
in the Baroque Era
(1600–1750)

Chapter 4
Ornamentation
in the Classical Era
(1750–1830)

Foreword

There has long been a need for a book that explains ornaments as they are used in each of the style periods of music. This book answers that need clearly and concisely.

In discussing ornamentation with hundreds of piano teachers over the past 50 years, I have encountered many who simply threw up their hands and said something like, "I have never understood all of these little signs and squiggles, and so I simply ignore them." Others said, "I believe that the execution of ornaments is so much a matter of personal taste that I simply play whatever I feel." These approaches are, of course, incorrect, and they rob the performer of the opportunity to use ornaments in their proper, highly functional, historical contexts.

The master composers, like Bach, Beethoven, Mozart, Chopin and others, knew the meanings of the ornamentation signs they chose to use. They knew which ones could be used in different ways, and which ones could be subject to several different realizations.

Fortunately for us, we have specific instructions from the pens of such composers as Henry Purcell, François Couperin, Jean-Henri d'Anglebert, J. S. Bach, C.P.E. Bach, Leopold Mozart, Frédéric Chopin and a host of other great artists and writers on the subject of music theory. These documents tell the performer which ornaments are acceptable in their music, and in which contexts they can best be used.

It is never enough to know only HOW an ornament should be played. The performer should have a clear idea about WHY each ornament should be played as recommended, and should know something even more subtle, and that is that *there can be more than one correct way to realize certain ornaments.* A performer who is properly schooled in the performance of ornaments should be able to look at a piece of music and tell exactly which ornaments are appropriate for use in any given passage by any composer of any era.

The GOOD NEWS is that the required knowledge for the proper performance of ornaments of all eras follows specific rules that are easy to grasp. When the student has learned these simple rules, playing ornaments becomes a pleasure. The performer knows exactly how the correct performance of the ornament can render the music more expressive and make the performance more pleasurable in every imaginable way.

In this book, Valery Lloyd-Watts and Carole L. Bigler have thoroughly explored the contours and contexts of all of the important ornaments of each major period, and have made the rules simple to learn and easy to remember.

Here, at last, we have a book that shows the relationships between the "pictures" of the most essential ornaments and their contours when they are realized. The ornaments have been identified by the authors as "pictographs." This means, essentially, that the ornament itself is an exact picture of the desired contour of the ornament. This clever approach makes the entire subject of ornamentation very clear and easy to learn.

I offer my congratulations to Valery Lloyd-Watts and Carole L. Bigler for presenting, for the first time, this original and imaginative approach to the understanding of the essential ornaments. I believe that their contributions will make the functions of ornaments, as well as the meaning of all of these signs, clear to every student, teacher and artist.

Willard A. Palmer

Preface

We wrote this book to help all musicians, regardless of instrument, understand ornamentation and be able to realize ornaments. We have done this by developing a logical step-by-step procedure that makes realizing an ornament and integrating it into a performance simple, stimulating and rewarding. Everyone using this book can be confident that the realizations will be accurate, historically correct and musically appropriate.

We are grateful to Willard A. Palmer for his contributions in the form of scholarly research on ornamentation and meticulous attention to detail. On a personal note, we are profoundly appreciative of his friendship, generosity of spirit and sense of humor.

Working through this complex subject and discovering how to make it easier for ourselves, our students and other teachers has been a challenging, exciting adventure. Writing a book is always a team effort and we gratefully acknowledge the patient assistance of Donald Watts for the many hours he spent helping to make the presentation logical, sequential and clear.

Sincere thanks to the helpful, exacting people at Alfred Publishing, starting with Iris and Morty Manus and continuing with Sharon Aaronson, E. L. Lancaster and Patrick Wilson. Also, a special note of thanks to Lauren Oppenheim of Princeton University Press.

We especially thank our husbands Donald Watts and William Bigler for their ongoing love and support.

Now it is our pleasure to share our work with you.

Valery Lloyd-Watts and Carole L. Bigler

Chapter 1
Answering Your Questions about Ornamentation

What is ornamentation?

Ornamentation is the practice of adding notes to a melody to allow music to be more expressive. This practice is also called "embellishment." Additional uses are to emphasize a note and to prolong its length because the earliest keyboard instruments had little capacity for sustaining a sound.

When did the practice of ornamenting melody begin?

There is evidence of ornamentation as early as the 14th century.

Why does this book begin with the Baroque era?

This book begins with the Baroque era because there is very little literature available prior to that time. During the Baroque, an enormous quantity of music was written, much of which has been edited by scholars and is readily available.

When did the Baroque era begin?

The Baroque era was so dominated by Johann Sebastian Bach that the dates of his birth and death (1685–1750) were used to define it. It is now generally accepted that the Baroque era began with a meeting in the early 1600s of a group in Italy called the Florentine Camerata.

The Florentine Camerata met to examine expressiveness in music and to discover ways of allowing a performer more freedom. It also examined the functions of ornaments that were expected to be added by performers.

What is an ornament?

An ornament is a set of *auxiliary* notes associated with a *main* note. Before an ornament can be performed, it must be *realized*. To realize an ornament, the notes of the ornament and their time values must be precisely specified.

How does an ornament make music more expressive?

All ornaments make music more expressive by using an auxiliary note to create a dissonant (harsh) sound that resolves to the consonant (agreeable) sound of the main note. This creates a sensation of tension and relief.

How is an ornament written?

Ornaments can be written in three ways:

1. As an auxiliary note in small print (♪) ahead of the main note, for example:

W. A. Mozart. Concerto for Violin No. 5, *K. 219, Adagio, measures 49–51*

2. As a special sign (ⵜ) over the main note, for example:

J. S. Bach. Sinfonia No. 8, *measure 1*

3. As a series of additional notes in small print, for example:

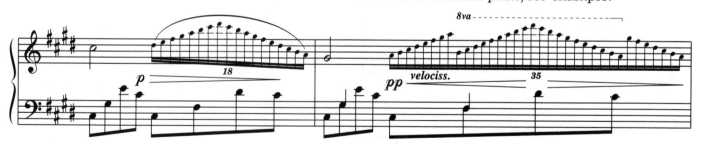

Frédéric Chopin. Nocturne in C-sharp Minor *(Posthumous), measures 58–59*

This latter example is a *fioritura*, which consists of a series of additional notes played against a series of accompaniment notes, with the configuration of the accompaniment notes specified by the composer (see chapter 7, page 55).

What is the most basic ornament?

The most basic of all ornaments is the *long appoggiatura* (pronounced ah-podge-ya-TOO-ra), in which the auxiliary and the main note are played only once. All other ornaments are constructed from this combination of notes. Its name comes from the Italian *appoggiare*, to lean.

How is the long appoggiatura written?

The long appoggiatura is always written as a small auxiliary note preceding the main note. The auxiliary note is often written as an eighth note (𝅘𝅥𝅮).

How is the long appoggiatura performed?

The auxiliary note is always played on the beat of the main note with emphasis (louder), borrowing its time from the main note, to which it is slurred (see chapter 3, page 27).

The following examples created by Willard A. Palmer, based on accepted practices of the Baroque era, illustrate how much more expressive music can be with the use of the long appoggiatura.

- **upper appoggiatura:** The auxiliary note usually repeats the note preceding the ornament or descends from a higher note. It is particularly expressive because it resembles a human sigh.

- **lower appoggiatura:** The auxiliary note almost always repeats the note preceding the ornament. It is expressive because it emphasizes the tension of the dissonance.

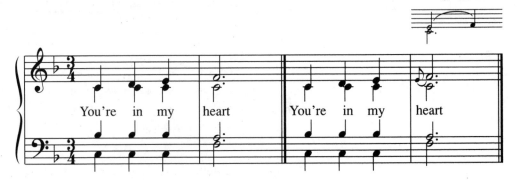

Ornamentation: A Question & Answer Manual

What are the other most common ornaments and how are they constructed?

The other most common ornaments are:

The mordent is constructed by following a main note with a lower appoggiatura; the turn by following an upper appoggiatura with a lower appoggiatura; and the trill by following an upper appoggiatura with other upper appoggiaturas in rapid succession. Each upper appoggiatura in a trill is called a repercussion. All other ornaments are more elaborate combinations of upper and lower appoggiaturas. *Except for the trill, ornaments have been realized the same way in all eras.*

How has the trill been treated differently?

In the Baroque era, all trills began on the auxiliary note, resolving to the main note (see chapter 3, page 29). In the Classical era, a turned ending became more common, but the practice of starting the trill on the upper auxiliary note continued (see chapter 4, page 41). In the Romantic era, some composers began to start the trill on the main note to prevent blurring the melodic or harmonic outlines (see chapter 5, pages 45–47). Romantic trills may begin on the auxiliary note *or* on the main note.

What was the effect of having trills begin in two different ways?

Having a choice caused confusion because it was not immediately obvious to a performer whether to begin on the auxiliary note or the main note. The confusion was aggravated in 1893, near the end of the Romantic era, when Edward Dannreuther emphasized the proposals of Hummel, Czerny and Spohr, which said that "the trill should begin on the main note for music of all eras in order not to blur the melodic line."[1] Thus, a practice begun in the Romantic era was applied retroactively to the Baroque and Classical eras!

Not all musicians accepted Dannreuther's proposal; one who did not was the great harpsichordist Wanda Landowska. She quoted, among others, François Couperin's *L'Art de toucher le Clavecin*, 1716–17 (The Art of Playing the Harpsichord), in which Couperin says, "A trill must always begin on the auxiliary note a tone or semitone higher than the [main] note upon which it is written."[2]

---

[1] Edward Dannreuther, *Musical Ornamentation* (New York: E. F. Kalmus, n.d.), part 1, 165; part 2, 112, 137.

[2] François Couperin, *L'Art de toucher le Clavecin* (The Art of Playing the Harpsichord), ed. and trans. Margery Halford (Van Nuys, CA: Alfred Publishing Co., Inc., 1974), 38.

Later, in the 20th century, authentic Baroque performance practices, along with the correct execution of Baroque ornaments, were reestablished, beginning with the pioneering efforts of Arnold Dolmetsch in his book *The Interpretation of the Music of the XVII and XVIII Centuries, Revealed by Contemporary Evidence*. Dolmetsch's work was continued by his son, Carl, and by his student Robert Donington in the book *The Interpretation of Early Music*. Also important is Donington's *A Performer's Guide to Baroque Music*.

Is there a fundamental principle to follow in realizing an ornament?

Yes, ornaments must be realized according to the composer's intentions and the conventions of the era in which the music was written. In chapters 3, 4, 5 and 6, proper performance practice of ornaments in the Baroque, Classical, Romantic and Contemporary eras is discussed.

Is it necessary to understand the interrelationships of art, architecture and music to realize ornaments correctly?

No, but understanding these relationships and how they have changed over the centuries has a powerful effect on the way the ephemeral shapes of the music can be perceived. Accordingly, in chapter 2 an overview of how art and architecture influenced the development of music is presented.

Summary

1. The practice of adding notes to a melody is called *ornamentation.*

2. The Baroque era began in the early 1600s with meetings of the Florentine Camerata, a group that met to examine how to make music more expressive.

3. An ornament is a set of *auxiliary* notes associated with a *main* note. Before an ornament can be performed, it must be realized.

4. The chief purpose of an ornament is to allow music to be more expressive. This is achieved by creating a dissonant (harsh) sound that resolves to a consonant (agreeable) sound, thus creating a sensation of tension and relief.

5. The most common ornaments are: the *long appoggiatura,* the *mordent,* the *turn* and the *trill.*

6. Ornaments must be realized according to the composer's intentions and the conventions of the era in which the music was written.

Chapter 2

An Overview of the Influence of Art and Architecture on the Development of Music

What is the interrelationship among art, architecture and music in the Baroque era?[3]

In Baroque art, architecture and music, tiny details are repeated again and again, but always with slight changes. Contrast is important. Notice the decorations on the case of the great organ of the Baroque church at Passau, Austria (example 2.1).

Example 2.1. The great organ of the Baroque church at Passau, Austria

The decorations consist of tiny curved patterns repeated over and over again. These little designs are counterbalanced and contrasted with the long, tubular organ pipes. Each detail of the architectural design contributes to the total effect, which is massive, elaborate, majestic, and, indeed, overwhelming in its grandeur.

---

[3] Willard A. Palmer and Margery Halford, eds., *The Baroque Era: An Introduction to the Keyboard Music* (Van Nuys, CA: Alfred Publishing Co., Inc., 1976).

The same attention to detail and the intricacy of small and large designs is reflected in Baroque music. The tiny design in the organ case may be said to correspond to the short Baroque *motive*, or musical idea, that appears throughout each piece, always recognizable but containing little changes to keep the ear interested. The pieces must be performed so that the motive is instantly identifiable. This is accomplished by giving it the same articulation (e.g., legato, staccato or portato) each time. The little motives fit together into longer phrases that are concluded by cadences.

The contrasts between curved, rounded forms and vertical shapes like pillars can be likened to contrasts between legato, staccato and portato notes. In music, stepwise progressions tend to be legato, and syncopations and wide leaps tend to be portato or staccato.

The contrasts between sharp angles and curved shapes, making beautiful patterns of light and shadow, find their analogies in the different tempos of the movements of a suite and in sharply contrasting dynamics. The accentuation of dissonances, especially in the ornaments, adds light and shade to Baroque music.

The irregularity of many Baroque designs finds a musical corollary in motives and phrases of irregular lengths and in rhythm patterns that often begin with an upbeat instead of a downbeat.

The Theory of Affects

The theory of affects (*Affectenlehre*) was an elaborate system that set forth ways in which emotion can be expressed through music. During the Baroque era, all art was concerned with its power to arouse and affect a person's emotional response. The theory defined which emotions were affected by specific rhythm patterns or harmonic progressions. It was the composer's responsibility to write the appropriate patterns of rhythm and harmony into the music and the performer's responsibility to interpret each affect or emotion so that the listener would immediately experience the desired reaction.

"Good Taste"

Baroque composers left much to the judgment of the performer (tempo, dynamics, phrasing, articulation, ornamentation, etc.). They relied on the knowledge and skill of the performer to perceive and execute their intentions. As contemporaries, performers were relied upon to fulfill the composer's wishes.

Two classes of ornaments developed during this period:

1. *Wilkürlich*: ornaments freely improvised by the performer.

2. *Wesentlich*: essential ornaments. These included the ornaments that were used so frequently that signs were developed for them (see the table of ornaments, page 26) and the cadential trill. For most cadences, a trill was obligatory regardless of whether its sign was used, and it was mandatory for certain cadential rhythm formulas such as:

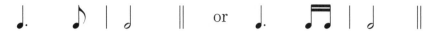

How have art, architecture and music in the Classical era changed from that of the Baroque era?[4]

The freely decorated, elaborate style of the Baroque era eventually gave way to the more restrained and formal approach of the Classical era. The beauty of the ancient Greek and Roman temples, many of which were excavated during these years, was seen as an ideal form of architecture.

The balance, symmetry and strong contrasts of geometrical shapes with subtle decorations were considered to be more tasteful than the excessively ornate, rococo structures popular in the Baroque era (example 2.2).

Example 2.2. The graceful, balanced symmetry of Classical architecture is seen in the Brandenburg Gate, Berlin, built 1788–91.

At the end of the Baroque period, the most popular form of keyboard composition was the *suite*, composed principally of a series of dance movements such as Allemande, Courante, Sarabande, Minuet and Gigue. Of these movements, the Minuet and Trio, with its balanced and contrasting sections, was most compatible with the Classical ideal. Consequently, it was one of the few dance forms that remained popular throughout the Classical era and became a part of the most important Classical form, the three- or four-movement sonata.

---

[4] Willard A. Palmer and Margery Halford, eds., *The Classical Era: An Introduction to the Keyboard Music* (Van Nuys, CA: Alfred Publishing Co., Inc., 1977).

Classicism in Architecture, Art and Music

The photo of the *Festsaal* (festival hall) of the Weimar Castle (example 2.3) presents the eye with restrained elegance and balanced grace that appear so natural and unforced that nothing could be added or omitted to make the effect more pleasing. The clear, unbroken straight lines that frame the *Festsaal* of the Weimar Castle are contrasted with the small, straight frames of the ceiling patterns. The modest decoration in these small frames is perfectly balanced by the decorations above the columns. The columns themselves are straight, unbroken lines, except for the simple Ionic *capitals* (the scroll decorations at the top). They serve to support the room and counterbalance the lines of the walls. The smooth, shiny floor reflects the ceiling. The openings between the columns highlight the heavy *frieze* (ornamental bands) above them. The interruptions of the doors and statues at the end of the room make the simplicity and clarity of the long lines even more elegant. The basic characteristics of the architecture of the interior of the *Festsaal* are also noticeable in the exteriors of churches and public buildings built in many countries during this period. Broad shoulder strips, deep porches supported by massive, formal columns, and walls pierced by elegant tall windows and doors are all part of Classical design.

Example 2.3. Festsaal (festival hall),
Castle of Weimar (Germany).
Built in 1802 by H. Gentz.

In the painting *Oath of the Horatii* by Jacques Louis David (example 2.4), the three swords in the center are balanced by the three curved arches of the background. The three strong sons on the left, with their beautifully proportioned bodies and virile masculinity, are counterbalanced by the three weeping women huddled and draped on the right. The starkness of the walls and floor, bare of decoration, is relieved by the geometrical designs of their building stones. The central, commanding figure of the father unites the picture, reemphasizing strength and control. Many Classical painters achieved graceful balance by contrasts of similar types. The focal point, like the most important theme in a composition, is often counterbalanced by a second subject of a completely different character, and these materials are highlighted and surrounded by objects of various sizes, colors, textures and designs.

Example 2.4.
Oath of the Horatii *(1784), by Jacques Louis David*
(Toledo Museum of Art).

These basic, Classical features are expressed in music in simple, flowing, beautiful melodies that move toward predictable cadences. Contrasting melodies are used to counterbalance one another. The modest patterning and subtle decoration in Classical architecture and painting find musical counterparts in bass configurations such as the *Alberti bass* and in elegant but rather sparse ornamentation. The strength of buildings and of central characters in painting are reflected in music by strong tonic-dominant harmony. The play of light and shadow finds its correspondence in modulations and sudden accents. The delicate contrasts and reflections of nature can be likened to the crescendos and diminuendos that add the equivalent of light and shade to music. Above all, perfect balance in all its many styles becomes most important in music in the sonata-allegro form. Thus, the sonata-allegro form may be said to transmute the basic features of classical design into sound.

The New Classical Performer: From "Co-Creator" to "Re-Creator"

The development of the pianoforte (example 2.5) exerted such a great influence on composers that the style of writing for keyboard changed in many important respects. The new pianoforte had the expressive capabilities of crescendo and diminuendo. It could produce delicate shadings of contrasting dynamics and sudden accents and could create both loud and soft sounds. This enabled the performer to bring out a melodic line while supporting and accompanying it with a softer, harmonic bass. The bass was the foundation in Baroque music, but in Classical music the melody assumed primary importance.

Example 2.5. Pianoforte built by Robert Stodart, London, 1790 (the Smithsonian Institution). Note the elegant, simple and restrained Classical lines, in spite of its resemblance to a Baroque harpsichord.

The pedal that raised the dampers off the strings was a completely new invention. It allowed richer harmonies to be achieved, because tones could continue to sound even after the fingers left the keys. The hammer and escapement mechanism of the piano was another important contribution to musical style. For the first time, the volume of a legato melody could be changed while being played. In fact, the new action made these legato connections sound so much like singing that playing in a "singing style" (*cantabile*) became a requirement for performing in "good taste."

With such an expressive instrument, the addition of ornaments to heighten expression became less essential and finally so "out of taste" as to be condemned. Furthermore, by the end of the Classical period, composers began to consider the addition of notes by a performer unpardonable. The performer was no longer expected to be "co-creator" with the composer. Good taste demanded that the composer's written text be followed faithfully, so that the music was recreated as nearly as possible, just as the composer conceived it.

How have art, architecture and music in the Romantic era changed from that of the Classical era?[5]

In an age when common people became recognized as individuals with emotions and needs of their own, it was natural that music and other art forms would begin to break away from the restraint and balance of the Classical era.

In the portrait of the poet Johann Wolfgang von Goethe (example 2.6), Romantic characteristics are clearly conveyed by the windswept hair, the casually wrapped garments clasped about the shoulders, and the vague, shadowed figures behind the poet. Formal balance and symmetry have no place in this painting. Its purpose is to illuminate the poetic nature of the man.

Example 2.6. Romantic portrait of Johann Wolfgang von Goethe, whose poems inspired Beethoven, Schubert and many others.

Composers reacted to the new freedom and emotionalism of the age by creating new forms for their compositions and by extending the limits of existing forms. The new forms reflected everyone's most personal emotions and longing for the beautiful and the truly unattainable.

Two distinct but complementary types of Romantic music developed: small and lyrical works, and huge and dramatic works, as illustrated by these contrasting lists of descriptive words.

Small and Lyrical	Huge and Dramatic
emotional	*fantastic*
sensitive	*dramatic*
poetic	*flamboyant*
dreamy	*heroic*
vague	*tragic*
melancholy	*intense*
yearning	*tempestuous*
sentimental	*colossal*

---

[5] Willard A. Palmer and Margery Halford, eds., *The Romantic Era: An Introduction to the Piano Music* (Van Nuys, CA: Alfred Publishing Co., Inc., 1978).

Those who wrote nationalistic music appealed to the deeply rooted patriotism in every individual. Listeners could weep or cheer or exalt or pine sentimentally with the composer, and their favorite dreams could be indulged in harmlessly as the music engulfed them. No longer under the patronage of either the Court or the Church, the composer became an important element of the social world, both as performer at concerts and as honored guest in fashionable homes.

The practice of giving explicit instructions to the performer, begun late in the Classical era, was now expanded. Composers wrote meticulous performance directions indicating tempo, dynamics, phrasing and style in the score, and ornaments were commonly incorporated into the melodic line rather than written as symbols.

The Influence of the Piano on the Romantic Era

The piano was the perfect instrument for the era of Romanticism. It already had the ability to produce a wide range of volume, but as the frame was strengthened, the hammers made larger and heavier, and the strings placed under greater tension, it became a thundering giant, capable of expressing the most violent raging (example 2.7). Because of the infinite control of touch that it now offered, the piano could also express the tenderest and most delicate sentimentalism through its caressing pianissimos. The damper pedal helped influence composers to write long, legato melodies and the slur began to take on its modern legato meaning. Regardless of how widely spaced the melody and harmony, or how intricate the movement of each part, with the damper pedal they could all be blended into a richly harmonic fabric that ideally suited the new chromatic chord progressions that the Romantic composers used so freely.

Example 2.7. Ornate grand piano by Erard,
built around 1830.

Ornamentation: A Question & Answer Manual

At concerts the piano was turned sideways so that the performer's profile could be seen and the audience could watch his or her hands. It was during the Romantic era that the solo concert became common, and the performer became a hero to the audience. Here was the opportunity for the artist to display the full range of his or her technical and interpretive abilities. Virtuosity reached almost unbelievable heights.

As soon as the upright piano (example 2.8) was developed, it became instantly popular, and many homes had one. Transcriptions of orchestral and ensemble works were printed almost before the premiere performances were heard, and composers wrote short, lyrical pieces with modest technical demands to meet the growing need for emotionally appealing music that everyone could learn to play. Publishers produced what Hector Berlioz was reputed to have called "an avalanche of romances, a torrent of airs and variations," to supply the insatiable demand.

Example 2.8. Pleyel upright piano with decorative handles, inlays and built-in candelabra.

The piano became the center of entertainment in the home. The family gathered around the instrument in the evening to listen and to sing. The *soiree*, to which guests were invited for musical entertainment, became one of the most popular forms of recreation.

Extravagantly gilded and decorated pianos built in various fantastic shapes, with such features as built-in candelabra, sliding racks that could be pulled out for holding candles or lamps, ornate handles for moving the instruments, and as many as eight pedals for producing various novel effects poured from hundreds of factories. One of the first upright pianos, built by Broadwood of London (example 2.9), housed the vertical strings in a curtained case almost nine feet tall. This top-heavy construction was soon abandoned in favor of a design more similar to the modern upright.

Example 2.9.
Upright piano by Broadwood.

A Romantic Setting for Romantic Performances

Grandiose concert halls (example 2.10) provided appropriate settings for Romantic operas, which were presented with extravagant costumes and no small amount of melodrama. Here Franz Liszt, Anton Rubinstein, Sigismond Thalberg and dozens of other virtuosos also dazzled audiences with their pianistic fireworks. In the concert hall shown, the super-violinist Nicolò Paganini played with such incredible skill that many of his amazed listeners believed he was in league with the devil. In the same hall, Hector Berlioz's *Symphonie fantastique* had its first performance. Paganini was so overwhelmed by this symphony that he made Berlioz a gift of 20,000 francs (about $4,000) as a token of his esteem. It was an age of drama and flair, sumptuousness and extravagance.

Example 2.10. Concert hall at the Conservatory of Music, Paris.

How have art, architecture and music in the Contemporary era changed from that of the Romantic era?[6]

Each era is, to some degree, a reaction against the previous one. A new musical epoch is a result of the belief that it is useless to explore further the style and forms of the previous era.

---

[6] Willard A. Palmer and Amanda Vick Lethco, eds., *Introduction to the Masterworks for the Piano* (Van Nuys, CA: Alfred Publishing Co., Inc. 1976).

In the 20th century, composers have been forced to seek new forms and even new tonal systems, since the musical possibilities of the diatonic system had been carried to their utmost boundaries during the previous century. Modern composers have not been united in an effort to move in any one particular direction, but rather, have attempted in many ways to free themselves from the limitations of traditional tonality, form and rhythmic notation.

Musical *Impressionism*, a term borrowed from the veiled and vague forms of Impressionistic paintings, was embodied in the works of Erik Satie, Claude Debussy and Maurice Ravel. It is characterized by the use of ancient church modes and by whole-tone scales that obscure tonality, and by general vagueness of form, long, flowing melodies, free rhythms, and less emphasis on the bar line.

Arnold Schönberg devised a completely new system involving the use of each of the 12 tones within the octave of the chromatic scale with equal importance, to avoid any feeling of key whatever. This has its parallel in the art of the Abstract painters, such as Pablo Picasso and Georges Braque, who changed our perceptions about art. Schönberg's system attracted many followers among modern composers. Igor Stravinsky, one of the most famous of modern musicians, led the way to new, progressive trends with his highly dissonant harmony, polytonality, strongly percussive rhythms, unusual accentuations within the measure and frequent changes of time signature.

An important development of the 20th century was the revival of interest in polyphonic writing. Schönberg and Paul Hindemith were possibly the two most important figures in this area. Henry Cowell and Charles Ives experimented with groups of neighboring tones sounding together, called *tone clusters*. The 20th-century American composer Aaron Copland frequently employed American folk music and jazz rhythms in his works.

Music composed "by chance" is called *aleatory* music, from the Latin word *alea*, meaning the game of dice. Notes, rhythms and other elements are selected by chance so that the composer has little control over the music finally produced. The American composer John Cage and the German composer Karlheinz Stockhausen are among leading exponents of such music.

In recent years, there has been renewed interest in Baroque performance practices, including the license to contribute to the work almost as much as the composer. In jazz music, the performer may even contribute more, and in some recent music, the performer is given only a sort of outline, to which he or she may add a variety of rhythms or notes or other elements to create a composition.

Chapter 3
Ornamentation in the Baroque Era
(1600–1750)

Who was the most influential person on the subject of ornamentation in the Baroque era?

No single person can be credited as the most influential. The principles of ornamentation were influenced by many composers and can be traced as far back as Henry Purcell (1659–1695). Ornaments evolved gradually and ultimately were standardized during the Baroque era. The French composers were responsible for systemizing signs (*agréments*) to establish definite rules for ornamentation (e.g., Jean-Henri d'Anglebert's *Pièces de Clavecin*[7] [Pieces for Harpsichord] contains a comprehensive table of ornaments and François Couperin's *L'Art de toucher le Clavecin*[8] [The Art of Playing the Harpsichord] explains his notation of ornaments). The French agréments became the model used by all European musicians from J. S. Bach through the Classical era.

Whose system for realizing Baroque ornaments is most commonly used today?

Johann Sebastian Bach's system is the one most commonly used today. In the *Clavier-Büchlein vor Wilhelm Friedemann Bach* (Little Clavier Book for Wilhelm Friedemann Bach), written in 1720 for his nine-year-old son, Bach constructed a table of ornaments that codified all the important ornaments used in the Baroque era. Called the "Explication" ("Explication unterschiedlicher Zeichen, so gewisse Manieren artig zu spielen, andeuten"), it is the only such table ever prepared by Bach (example 3.1).[9]

---

[7] Jean-Henri d'Anglebert, *Pièces de Clavecin*, 1689 (Pieces for Harpsichord), quoted in Dannreuther, *Musical Ornamentation*, part 1, 95.

[8] Couperin, *L'Art de toucher*, 12.

[9] Willard A. Palmer, ed., *J. S. Bach: An Introduction to his Keyboard Music* (Van Nuys, CA: Alfred Publishing Co., Inc., 1973), 4.

*Example 3.1. Facsimile of the "Explication" in J. S. Bach's own handwriting.
Courtesy of the Yale University Music Library.*

J. S. Bach's Table of Ornaments

The "Explication" is also reproduced below, using modern notation and terminology rather than the mixture of Italian, German, French and Latin in Bach's autograph. This table of ornaments provides the fundamentals required to realize ornaments in music from the Baroque to the Romantic era!

EXPLANATION OF VARIOUS SIGNS, SHOWING HOW TO PLAY CERTAIN ORNAMENTS PROPERLY[10]

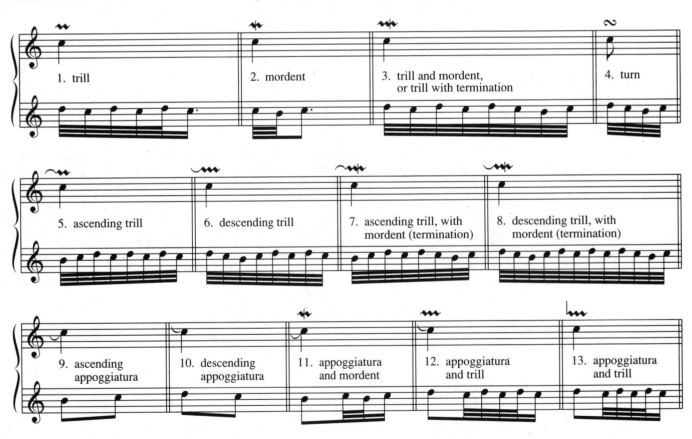

---

10 Willard A. Palmer, ed., *J. S. Bach: Inventions and Sinfonias* (Van Nuys, CA: Alfred Publishing Co., Inc., 1968), 4.

Ornamentation: A Question & Answer Manual

What is the key to understanding the table of ornaments?

The key to understanding the table of ornaments is to recognize that the ornaments are presented as *pictographs* that clearly and accurately describe what must happen in the performance of the music.

What are the ornaments?

Bach shows 13 ornaments, based on the appoggiatura, the trill, the mordent and the turn. The long appoggiatura (called the ascending and descending appoggiatura by Bach) is the most basic (see page 10).

- **long appoggiatura** (table of ornaments, examples 9 and 10)

In the pictograph, Bach uses a little *hook* below the note in example 9, which means the auxiliary note is a tone or a semitone below the main note, depending on the key of the passage, and usually takes half the duration of the main note. This is an example of a lower appoggiatura. In example 10, the hook is clearly *above* the note, which means the auxiliary note is a tone or a semitone above, depending on the key of the passage. This is an example of an upper appoggiatura.

Composers eventually began writing a small notehead instead of a hook. Consequently, the hook probably will not be seen in any printed editions. The small notehead was used in spite of the fact that all musicians of the day knew that the long appoggiatura had half the duration of the main note (see page 28). One question from present-day students is always "If it takes half the value of the note (for example, ♪), why did the composer write the little notehead?" Leopold Mozart, father of W. A. Mozart, supplies the answer somewhat obliquely in his *Treatise on the Fundamental Principles of Violin Playing*: "It is true that all the descending appoggiaturas could be set down in large print and divided within the bar. But if a violinist who knows not that the appoggiatura is written out, or who is already accustomed to befrill every note, happens on such, how will it fare with melody as well as harmony? I wager that such a violinist will add yet another long appoggiatura."[11] To paraphrase, those musicians who couldn't tell the difference between the auxiliary and the main note would probably add another ornament to the ornament!

Putting the auxiliary in small print was also helpful to a performer because it showed that the main note was clearly part of the harmony while the auxiliary note created the dissonance and was meant to be emphasized. If the two notes were written of equal size and time value, the second note might be mistaken for a passing tone.

---

[11] Leopold Mozart, *A Treatise on the Fundamental Principles of Violin Playing*, trans. Editha Knocker (London: Oxford University Press, 1951), 167.

J. S. Bach did nothing to indicate the value of the notes of his appoggiaturas, so one must use the general rules set forth by later composers, such as Carl Philipp Emanuel Bach[12] and Johann Joachim Quantz.[13]

1. The long appoggiatura is played on the beat. This means that the auxiliary note is played simultaneously with the accompaniment notes (the alto, tenor and bass notes in the following example were created by Willard A. Palmer):

2. The long appoggiatura usually takes half the time of the note that follows it, except when it is followed by a dotted note. It then usually takes two-thirds of the value of the main note (examples b, d and f below).[14]

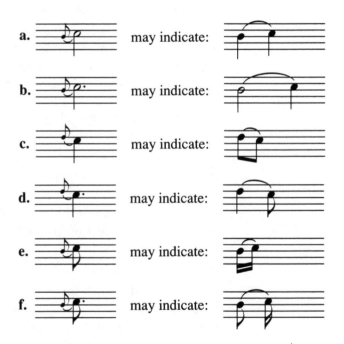

Note: The modern acciaccatura or "grace note" ( ) appears in many modern editions of the music of J. S. Bach. The appoggiatura with a cross stroke was never written by J. S. Bach and editions containing them are not accurate.[15]

[12] Carl Philipp Emanuel Bach, *Essay on the True Art of Playing Keyboard Instruments*, trans. William J. Mitchell (New York: W. W. Norton, 1949), 90.

[13] Johann J. Quantz, *Essay on a Method of Playing the Transverse Flute*, trans. Edward R. Reilly (London: Faber and Faber, 1976), 95.

[14] Palmer, *Bach: Inventions and Sinfonias*, 10.

[15] Willard A. Palmer, ed., *J. S. Bach: The Well-Tempered Clavier, Volume 1* (Van Nuys, CA: Alfred Publishing Co., Inc., 1981), 17.

The Baroque acciaccatura appears as a cross stroke between two chord-notes. The chord is arpeggiated and a dissonant note is added between two chord-notes in the place where the cross stroke appears. The notes of the chord are held, but the added dissonant note is instantly released:

- **trill** (table of ornaments, example 1)

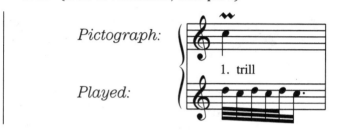

In the pictograph, Bach shows only ⚹ for the trill, but a trill may also be indicated by ⚹ or *tr*. Any of these signs may indicate a long or short trill. *All trills begin on the beat and all ordinary trills in Bach's music begin on the auxiliary (upper) note.* In addition to this use in the table of ornaments, this practice is verified in C.P.E. Bach's *Essay on the True Art of Playing Keyboard Instruments*[16] and in the writings of other well-known musicians of the early and late 18th century. In essence they state the objective of a trill is to create dissonance followed by resolution. When a trill begins on the consonant sound (the main note), the dissonance does not occur, and so the stated objective of the trill is not achieved. Trills are most effective when used on notes that descend from the previous upper second and are obligatory when a cadential formula occurs (see page 15).

The number of repercussions in a trill depends upon the time value of the main note, the tempo of the selection, and the skill and taste of the performer. *The minimum number of repercussions in a short trill is two.*

---

[16] C.P.E. Bach, *Essay on the True Art,* 100.

The following examples show the trill realized for different time values.[17]

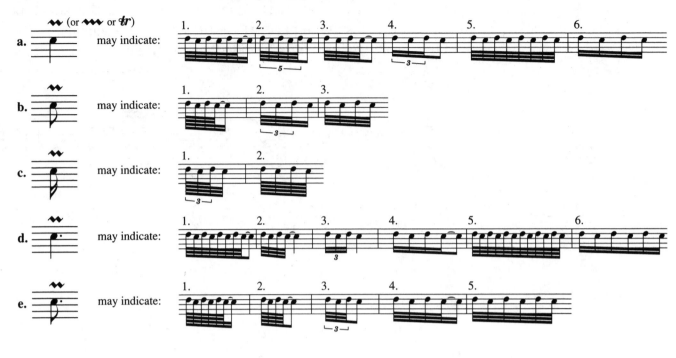

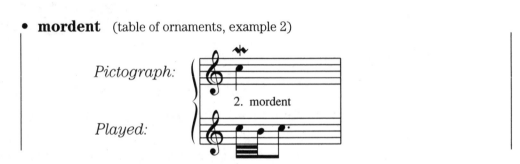

- **mordent** (table of ornaments, example 2)

Pictograph:

2. mordent

Played:

The pictograph indicates the drawing down of the sound by the stroke (|), which was surely made by the pen moving from the top to the bottom. So the sign ✶ places the dissonance on the lower auxiliary note between two strikings of the main notes.

The word *mordent* comes from the Latin *mordere*, which means to bite. Thus the mordent is a "biting" ornament that adds rhythmic accent and brilliance to notes.

The mordent is played on the beat—that is, it begins on the main note at exactly the instant when the main note is indicated to be played (never ahead of time) and moves *downward* quickly to "bite" the lower note and returns instantly to the main note. The mordent should be played as rapidly as possible.

Mordents are most effective when played on upward steps or leaps. They are also effective when used in the bass on a note just before the downward leap of an octave. C.P.E. Bach states in his *Essay on the True Art of Playing Keyboard Instruments* that "the mordent is an essential ornament that connects notes, fills them out, and makes them brilliant."[18]

[17] Palmer, *Bach: Inventions and Sinfonias*, 4–5.
[18] C.P.E. Bach, *Essay on the True Art*, 127.

The following examples show the mordent realized for different time values.[19]

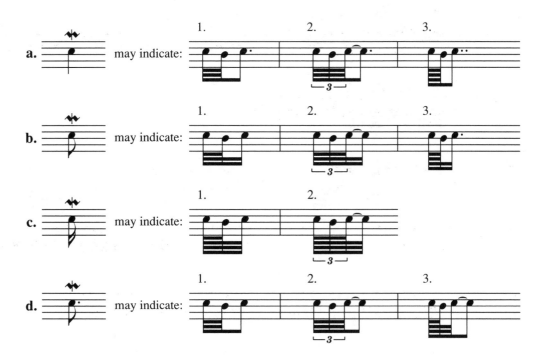

- **trill and mordent** (or trill with termination, trill with suffix, or trill with closing notes [table of ornaments, example 3])

Looking at the pictograph, a trill plus a mordent or suffix can be seen. The trill requires a minimum of two repercussions, with the suffix (or termination) consisting of two notes.

The trill may contain more than two repercussions, so the above example plus Bach's own written example from the table of ornaments (example 3) are consistent.

---

[19] Palmer, *Bach: Inventions and Sinfonias,* 5.

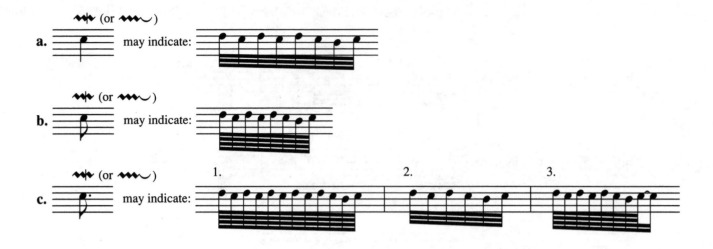

• **ascending trill** (table of ornaments, example 5)

Pictograph:

Played:

5. ascending trill

The pictograph shows: Approach the trill from below the main note, play the main note, then ascend to the upper auxiliary note and continue to trill as usual.

The contour line clearly describes the shapes created by the first two notes (the prefix, which is a lower appoggiatura) followed by a trill consisting of at least two repercussions (in this case, Bach has used three repercussions).

prefix └── trill ──┘

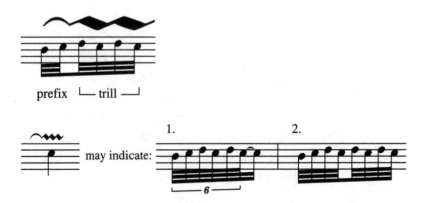

- **descending trill** (table of ornaments, example 6)

The pictograph shows: Approach the trill from the upper auxiliary note, play the main note, then play the lower auxiliary note, return via the main note and continue to trill as usual.

The contour line describes the shape created by the first four notes (the prefix, which can be recognized as a turn), followed by the trill, which requires at least two repercussions.

- **ascending trill with mordent as a termination**
  (table of ornaments, example 7)

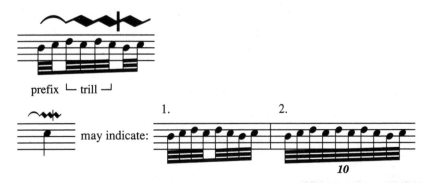

The pictograph of the ascending trill with mordent shows: Play the note below the main note, play the main note, then ascend to the upper note and trill for a minimum of two repercussions, then follow with the lower auxiliary and finish with the main note.

The contour line describes the shapes created by the first two notes (prefix, which is a lower appoggiatura), followed by the trill (two repercussions), ending with the lower auxiliary and main notes (a lower appoggiatura).

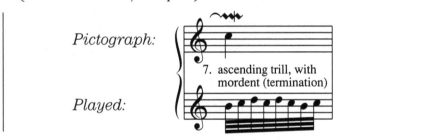

- **descending trill with mordent as a termination**
  (table of ornaments, example 8)

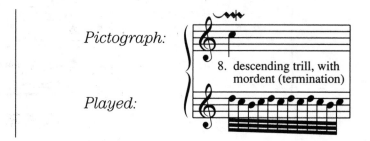

Pictograph:

8. descending trill, with
   mordent (termination)

Played:

The pictograph of the descending trill with mordent (termination) shows to play the upper note, then the main note, descend to the lower note, return via the main note to the upper note, and continue the repercussions until descending again to the lower note and finishing on the main note.

The contour line describes the shapes created by the first four notes (prefix, which can be recognized as a turn) followed by the trill (a minimum of two repercussions) and ending with the mordent (termination, which is a lower appoggiatura).

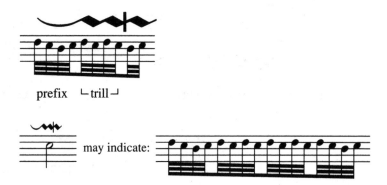

prefix └ trill ┘

may indicate:

- **appoggiatura and mordent** (table of ornaments, example 11)

Pictograph:

11. appoggiatura
    and mordent

Played:

As discussed previously (see page 27), the little hook below the note in the pictograph signifies the lower auxiliary note and must take half the time value of the main note, in this case an eighth note. The mordent fills the remaining eighth-note value with the main note, lower auxiliary and main note again.

- **appoggiatura and trill** (table of ornaments, example 12)

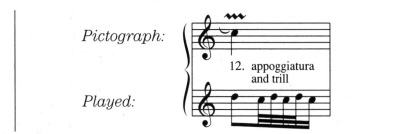

Pictograph:

Played:

12. appoggiatura and trill

The hook in the pictograph is above the note, so the note the hook represents will be the upper auxiliary note, taking half the value (an eighth note) of the main note. This note therefore acts also as the first note of the trill to follow. The trill employs the remaining eighth-note value. This sign is not used in present-day editions.

- **appoggiatura and trill** (table of ornaments, example 13)

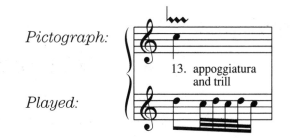

Pictograph:

Played:

13. appoggiatura and trill

The long downstroke on the pictograph means to linger on the first note of the trill (the upper note). This ornament contains exactly the same notes as the appoggiatura and trill sign shown in example 12. In many of the writings of the period, the authors state that the first note of a trill (the upper note which creates the dissonance) is to be strongly emphasized both in dynamic and by length.[20]

[20] Arnold Dolmetsch, *The Interpretation of the Music of the XVII and XVIII Centuries, Revealed by Contemporary Evidence* (London: Novello, 1915), 154–195.

- **turn** (table of ornaments, example 4)

Pictograph:

Played:

This pictograph again depicts exactly what to do:

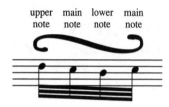

upper   main   lower   main
note   note   note   note

Play the upper note, then the main note, descend to the lower note and finish by playing the main note again. This is a combination of an upper appoggiatura followed by a lower appoggiatura.

Because the turn begins on the note above the main note, it often conveys a fleeting touch of expressive dissonance. In general, the note values of the turn are divided equally, but in performance beginning ones may be hurried along so there is time to hold the last note.

The following examples show the turn realized for different time values.

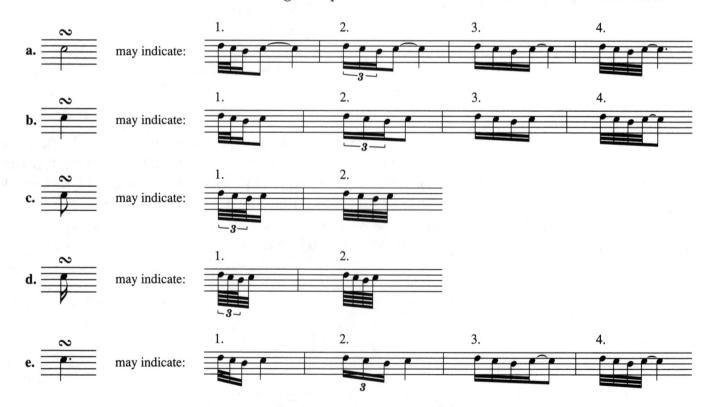

When the turn is placed *between* two notes, the turn is played after the principal note has been sounded. The rhythm of the turn must then be determined by the amount of time available for it. There are usually several acceptable solutions:

"The turn," wrote C.P.E. Bach, "is almost too obliging. It fits almost anywhere."[21] He added that it should not be used too frequently and that it is most effective when added to notes with short rhythm values.

• other ornaments

Now all the ornaments given by Bach in his table of ornaments have been examined. There are a few additional ornaments used in Baroque music that can be found in more exhaustive treatments on ornamentation, such as the prefaces to the first volume of the *Well-Tempered Clavier*, edited by Willard A. Palmer, and the complete *Inventions and Sinfonias* by J. S. Bach, edited by Willard A. Palmer.

In another practice of the Baroque era, the performer was free to invent an unlimited number of configurations around the melody. Fine Baroque performers relished such improvisations, and Baroque audiences expected and enjoyed them. This practice, called *free ornamentation*, challenged the skill and imagination of the performer; and those who did not add such embellishments, particularly when repeating a section, were considered dull and unimaginative. For information about free ornamentation, see chapter 8 (pages 58–63) and *The Baroque Era: An Introduction to the Keyboard Music*, edited by Willard A. Palmer and Margery Halford.

Does Bach give any instructions for applying the table of ornaments?

Yes, Bach provides instruction by example in the Applicatio. This short piece, which follows the table of ornaments in the *Clavier-Büchlein*, demonstrates most of the ornaments in correct context. The Applicatio with the ornaments realized by Willard A. Palmer follows.

---

[21] C.P.E. Bach, *Essay on the True Art*, 114.

Applicatio, BWV 994

from the *Little Clavier Book for W. F. Bach,*
realized by Willard A. Palmer

Ornamentation: A Question & Answer Manual

From Bach's use of the ornaments in the Applicatio, we can infer the following general rules for the mordent and the trill:

The mordent may be added to the first melody note of a piece or section of a piece, or to the first note of a clearly defined phrase. A mordent is best added to notes *ascending*

or in the *bass* on the highest note of a phrase or a motive, particularly when the following note is an octave lower.

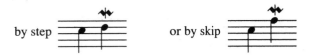

The trill may be added to notes *descending*

Summary

1. The greatest master of the Baroque era was Johann Sebastian Bach (1685–1750).

2. Bach's table of ornaments (1720) illustrates most of the commonly used ornaments.

3. The instructions for realizing the ornaments are in the form of pictographs that give clear and accurate descriptions of what must happen in the music.

4. All ornaments are played on the beat.

5. All trills begin on the upper auxiliary note.

Chapter 4
Ornamentation in the Classical Era
(1750–1830)

Who were the most influential persons on the subject of ornamentation in the Classical era?

Leopold Mozart, Wolfgang Amadeus Mozart, Franz Joseph Haydn and Carl Philipp Emanuel Bach are considered to be the most influential.

C.P.E. Bach's influence was most strongly felt, however, by the great composers of the Classical era. In 1753, in a book entitled *Essay on the True Art of Playing Keyboard Instruments*, he set forth his instructions for playing ornaments. These instructions correspond with the table of ornaments written by his father, J. S. Bach, specifically in that all ornaments are played on the beat and that "the trill always begins on the tone above the main note."[22] The young Bach wrote, "In composition and keyboard playing, I never had any other teacher than my father."[23]

During this time, composers began to follow C.P.E. Bach's suggestion that all ornamentation be written out on the page. But it was many years before performers entirely dropped the custom of spontaneously adding ornaments, especially in repeated sections and slow movements.

Did ornamentation in the Classical era differ from that of the Baroque era?

No, the sign for the appoggiatura changed, but not its execution.

How was the sign for the appoggiatura altered?

In the Baroque era, the auxiliary note was usually printed as a small eighth note, no matter what its *performance* time value was. C.P.E. Bach, following his father's teaching, suggested that the small note be written in its *actual* time value and that the value be subtracted from the value of the main note.[24] So great was his influence that almost all composers of the Classical era followed this practice.

---

[22] C.P.E. Bach, *Essay on the True Art,* 100.

[23] William S. Newman, trans., "Emanuel Bach's Autobiography," *Musical Quarterly* 51 (Summer 1965): 366.

[24] C.P.E. Bach, *Essay on the True Art,* 87.

To illustrate, the appoggiatura written as

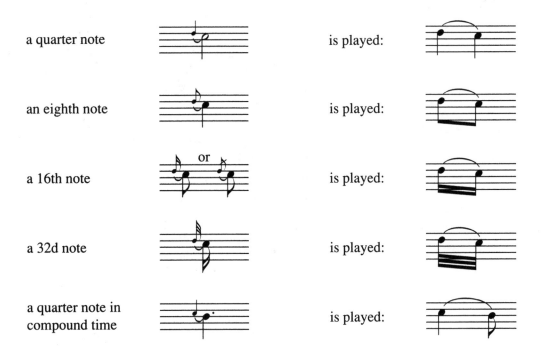

a quarter note		is played:	
an eighth note		is played:	
a 16th note	or	is played:	
a 32d note		is played:	
a quarter note in compound time		is played:	

The symbol ♪ is simply an old way of writing a 16th note (♬). Mozart was among the first to use the symbol with the cross stroke to indicate a 16th-note appoggiatura. It is played on the beat, for the value of a 16th note.

How was the trill performed?

Standard trills of the Classical era were identical to those of the Baroque era.[25] In the table of ornaments, Bach gives five examples of a trill without termination and three with termination (see page 26). Now, however, they most commonly ended with a turned ending (termination), whether or not the turned ending was printed in small or large notes:

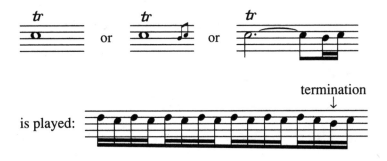

---

[25] Willard A. Palmer, ed., *W. A. Mozart: An Introduction to his Keyboard Works* (Van Nuys, CA: Alfred Publishing Co., Inc., 1974), 12.

What is the short appoggiatura?

The short appoggiatura is written as a small 16th or 32d note before a main note and is played very quickly, on the beat of the main note.[26] It is frequently found before a quick rhythmic group.

As the symbol ♪ is an old way of writing a 16th note (the cross stroke is used as an additional flag), the symbol 𝄽 is likewise an old way of writing a 32d note. The small note is played *on the beat* and is given its written value, which is subtracted from the following note, in accordance with the recommendations of C.P.E. Bach:

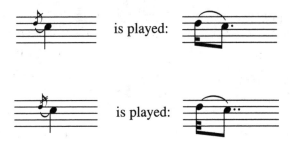

Summary

1. C.P.E. Bach's *Essay on the True Art of Playing Keyboard Instruments*, published in 1753, was the most influential writing on ornamentation in the Classical era.

2. Ornamentation in the Classical era is realized in the same way as in the Baroque era.

3. C.P.E. Bach suggested that all ornamentation be written out on the page by the composer.

4. C.P.E. Bach emphasized his father's teaching that the auxiliary note of the long appoggiatura be printed in its actual time value. This value is subtracted from the value of the main note.

5. The trill still begins on the upper auxiliary note, as in the Baroque era, but trills were usually played with a turned ending (termination).

---

26 Ibid., 11.

Chapter 5
Ornamentation in the Romantic Era
(1830–1900)

Who was the most influential person on the subject of ornamentation in the Romantic era?

Surprisingly, Johann Nepomuk Hummel of the Classical era exerted the most powerful influence on Romantic ornamentation through his widely used method book for piano. In his book *A Complete Theoretical and Practical Course of Instructions on the Art of Playing the Piano Forte, Commencing with the Simplest Elementary Principles and Including Every Information Requisite to the Most Finished Style of Performance,*[27] he proposed that for his own compositions trills be played beginning on the main note rather than on the upper auxiliary. Chief among his reasons was that the melody is more apparent when the trill begins on the melody note. He acknowledged that until 1828, when his book was published, trills were generally begun on the upper auxiliary.

To place Hummel's ideas in historical context, it is instructive to review the evolutionary process that began in the early 19th century. In a famous method book entitled *Introduction to the Art of Playing on the Piano Forte*, Muzio Clementi stressed the importance of beginning most trills on the upper note but allowing for "transient shakes" beginning on the main note, and for long trills beginning on the main note to preserve the legato in certain passages.[28]

Beethoven learned to play ornaments in the manner prescribed by C.P.E. Bach, and in teaching he used both C.P.E. Bach's *Essay on the True Art of Playing Keyboard Instruments* and Clementi's *Introduction to the Art of Playing on the Piano Forte*. Beethoven was quite aware of the problems that might be created by the allowance of Clementi's exceptions, and in passages in his own compositions where there might be confusion he often inserted a small note indicating the starting note of the trill. In the absence of such a note, it is reasonably certain that the trill begins on the upper note.

---

[27] Johann Nepomuk Hummel, *Ausführliche theoretisch-practische Anweisung zum Piano-Forte Spiel, vom ersten Elementar-Unterrichte an bis zur vollkomensten Ausbildung,* 1828 (A Complete Theoretical and Practical Course of Instructions on the Art of Playing the Piano Forte, Commencing with the Simplest Elementary Principles and Including Every Information Requisite to the Most Finished Style of Performance), quoted in Dannreuther, *Musical Ornamentation*, part 2, 145.

[28] Robert Donington, *The Interpretation of Early Music* (New York: W. W. Norton, newly revised and enlarged version, 1989), 256.

Also in this historical context, since Carl Maria von Weber died in 1826, Ludwig van Beethoven in 1827, and Franz Schubert in 1828, Hummel's decision probably did not affect the way these other composers wanted their trills played. One can assume these composers were in agreement with Clementi's practices, which stated that trills *generally* begin on the upper note *but that trills following stepwise motion in a legato melody, or very short trills on passing tones, could begin on the main note.*[29]

After Hummel's book was published in the year following Beethoven's death, many famous artists (including Carl Czerny, who was a great admirer of Hummel) influenced others by playing Beethoven's trills incorrectly—but not because Beethoven had allowed Czerny to play them that way. Czerny himself relates that when he played the Sonata in C Minor, Op. 13 ("Pathétique") for Beethoven, the master agreed to take him as a pupil with the proviso that he obtain a copy of C.P.E. Bach's *Essay* and bring it with him to the first lesson.[30] Beethoven probably wanted to point out to Czerny that the trills in this sonata must be played beginning on the upper note.

What happened as a result of Hummel's proposals?

Many composers, including Johannes Brahms, Edvard Grieg, Franz Liszt, Felix Mendelssohn and Robert Schumann, adopted his proposal; but others, including Frédéric Chopin, John Field, Franz Schubert and Carl Maria von Weber did not. Perhaps the most important consequence was that within 75 years, writers and musicians of the Romantic era began to apply Hummel's proposals to music of the Baroque and Classical eras (see chapter 1, page 11). In doing so, they violated the fundamental principle that ornaments must be realized according to the composer's intentions and the conventions of the era in which the music was written.

---

[29] Muzio Clementi, *Introduction to the Art of Playing on the Piano Forte* (London: Clementi, Banger, Hyde, Collard and Davis, 1801; reprint of first edition, second issue, New York: Da Capo Press, 1974), 11.

[30] Oscar George Sonneck, ed., *Beethoven: Impressions by his Contemporaries* (New York: G. Schirmer, Inc., 1926), 27.

- **acciaccatura**[32]

Acciaccatura (a-CHACK-a-too-ra), from the Italian meaning, "to crush," has been familiarly but incorrectly anglicized to denote a rapid appoggiatura of the ordinary kind (a short appoggiatura). The acciaccatura is played almost simultaneously with the main note and the term "simultaneous appoggiatura" is to be preferred.

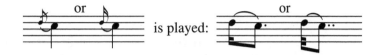

- **turn**

When the turn appears over the main note, it begins immediately, on the upper auxiliary, on the beat of the main note.

When the turn appears after the main note, the main note is played before beginning the turn.

- **the trill in the music of Beethoven, Chopin, Field, Schubert and Weber**

The trill generally begins on the upper auxiliary note. A termination is usually added, whether indicated or not.

---

[31] Palmer and Halford, *The Romantic Era.*

[32] Stanley Sadie, ed., *The New Grove Dictionary of Music and Musicians* (London: Macmillan, 1989), s.v. "Ornaments" by Robert Donington.

The trill may begin slowly and increase in speed. When the trill is played legato with the preceding upper or lower second, it can begin on the main note.

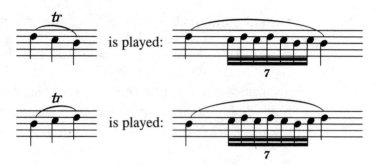

A small note on the same line or space as the trilled note indicates that the trill begins on that note (the main note).

The sign ⌁ is frequently used to indicate a short trill beginning on the upper auxiliary.

The same sign can indicate a passing or transient trill, especially in rapid, descending passages.

- **the trill in the music of Brahms, Grieg, Liszt, Mendelssohn and Schumann**

The trill generally begins on the main note. A termination is usually added, whether indicated or not. The trill may begin slowly and increase in speed.

A small note on the line or space a second higher than the trilled note indicates that the trill begins on that note (the upper auxiliary).

This applies to all other composers from the Romantic era to the present.

The same sign ❧ can indicate a passing or transient trill.

- **mordent**

The mordent disappeared from general use in the music of the Romantic era.

Summary

1. In 1828, Johann Nepomuk Hummel wrote his book *A Complete Theoretical and Practical Course of Instructions on the Art of Playing the Piano Forte, Commencing with the Simplest Elementary Principles and Including Every Information Requisite to the Most Finished Style of Performance.* In it he proposed that trills be played beginning on the main note, chiefly because the melody is more apparent when the trill begins on the melody note.

2. Hummel's ideas powerfully influenced Brahms, Grieg, Liszt, Mendelssohn and Schumann.

3. Hummel's ideas did not influence Chopin, Field, Schubert or Weber.

4. The short appoggiatura was modified to become the acciaccatura.

5. The Romantic composers were now explicit in their instructions on how the music was to be played.

6. Ornaments were often incorporated into the melodic line rather than written as symbols.

Chapter 6

Ornamentation in the Contemporary Era (1900–present)

Who is the most influential person on the subject of ornamentation in the present era?

The composer is the most influential person. Most composers indicate their intentions precisely so that realizing ornaments is no longer left to the discretion of the performer.

How are ornaments indicated?

- Most musical ornaments have become obsolete. The composers write explicitly the notes they wish to have played.

- Trills begin on the main note and on the beat, as in most music of the Romantic era, unless the composer clearly indicates otherwise.

- The long appoggiatura is no longer written as an ornament.

- The short appoggiatura (or acciaccatura) is generally played ahead of the beat or simultaneously with the main note, a practice evolving largely from confusion regarding the performance of this ornament during the Romantic era.

- Turns and mordents, when they are used, are generally written as ordinary notes.

Chapter 7

A Procedure for Realizing Ornaments and Strategies for Effective Practicing

Expressive performance of an ornament requires technically correct realization of the ornament as well as accurate and smooth integration of the realized ornament into the score. Presented in this chapter is a procedure for realizing an ornament, expressed as a sequence of questions and actions. Then, strategies for analyzing and practicing ornaments are discussed, making it possible to perform an embellished melodic line accurately and expressively.

A Procedure for Realizing an Ornament

To realize an ornament, answer the following questions:

1. Who is the composer and what is the era?

2. What is the name of the ornament?

3. What is the time signature of the passage of music?

4. How many beats or subdivisions of a beat must the ornament fill?

5. How should the rhythm be subdivided? (See the Table for Counting and Subdivision of Beats, page 51, and Write the Counting in the Score, page 52.)

Action: Write the counting in the score.

6. Does the ornament begin on the auxiliary note or the main note?

7. How many notes must the ornament have? (Refer to chapters 3, 4, 5 and 6.)

   a. If the ornament is a trill, how many repercussions will (or can) you play?

   b. How will you end the trill? (Tied to the next note? With a termination?) (See chapter 3, page 30 and chapter 4, page 41).

Action: Write the realization in the score.

Answering these questions will help you realize any ornament correctly in any era.

In the next section is a discussion on how to integrate ornaments into a score and how to practice ornaments so that they can be performed accurately at tempo.

There is more to performing an ornament than simply inserting its technically correct realization into the score. To perform an embellished melodic line expressively involves several elements:

- accurate note playing

- precise rhythm

- tempo rubato

- appropriate dynamics

The element most likely to be disturbed by the additional notes of an ornament is rhythmic precision. To ensure smooth integration and facile performance of ornaments (so that "grace" notes will not be "disgrace" notes, to paraphrase Artur Schnabel),[33] we recommend five steps:

1. Count out loud while practicing.

2. Write the counting in the score.

3. Measure all trills to master them.

4. Use a metronome to ensure precise rhythm.

5. Begin learning rhythmically complicated passages at a comfortable speed and gradually increase to performance tempo.

A discussion of each of these strategies follows.

Step 1: Count out loud while practicing.

Counting out loud is one of the most helpful practicing strategies. It requires extra concentration, but the payoff is well worth it. Using the following Table for Counting and Subdivision of Beats, tap and count the rhythm out loud as a separate exercise to become comfortable with changing rhythms smoothly between groups of two, three and four notes—for example, between eighth notes, triplet eighth notes and 16th notes.

---

[33] Konrad Wolff, *The Teachings of Artur Schnabel: A Guide to Interpretation* (London: Faber and Faber, 1972), 104.

TABLE FOR COUNTING AND SUBDIVISION OF BEATS

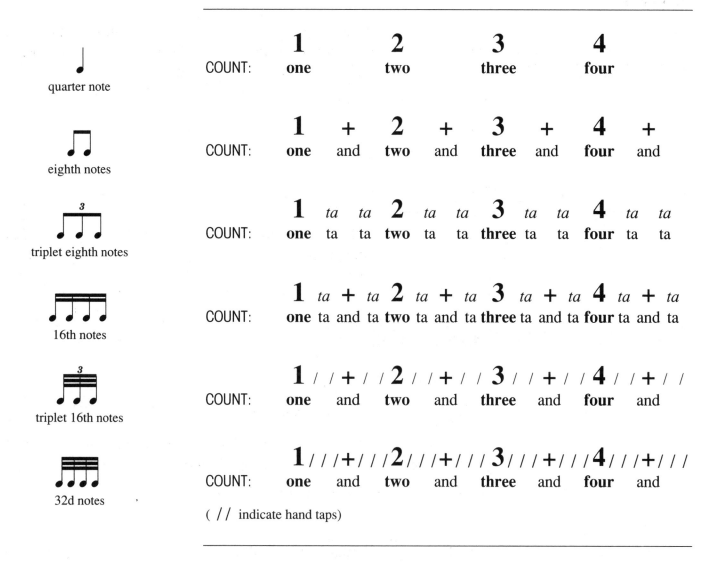

quarter note

eighth notes

triplet eighth notes

16th notes

triplet 16th notes

32d notes

	1		2		3		4	
COUNT:	**one**		**two**		**three**		**four**	

	1	+	2	+	3	+	4	+
COUNT:	**one**	and	**two**	and	**three**	and	**four**	and

	1	*ta*	*ta*	2	*ta*	*ta*	3	*ta*	*ta*	4	*ta*	*ta*
COUNT:	**one**	ta	ta	**two**	ta	ta	**three**	ta	ta	**four**	ta	ta

	1	*ta*	+	*ta*	2	*ta*	+	*ta*	3	*ta*	+	*ta*	4	*ta*	+	*ta*
COUNT:	one	ta	and	ta	**two**	ta	and	ta	**three**	ta	and	ta	**four**	ta	and	ta

	1 / /	+ / /	2 / /	+ / /	3 / /	+ / /	4 / /	+ / /
COUNT:	**one**	and	**two**	and	**three**	and	**four**	and

	1 / / /	+ / / /	2 / / /	+ / / /	3 / / /	+ / / /	4 / / /	+ / / /
COUNT:	**one**	and	**two**	and	**three**	and	**four**	and

(/ / indicate hand taps)

Say "1, 2, 3, 4" for quarter notes; "1-and, 2-and, 3-and, 4-and" for eighth notes; "1-ta-ta, 2-ta-ta," etc., for triplet eighth notes; 1-ta-and-ta, 2-ta-and-ta" for 16th notes; and "1-and, 2-and" for triplet 16th and 32ds because at these smaller values the tapping becomes too fast to say a separate syllable for each tap. Use the syllable "ta" for triplets and 16th notes because it is the easiest sound to enunciate quickly. (Trumpeters use this sound for articulation.) When practicing the patterns on the chart as a rhythm exercise, the left and right hands alternate taps.

To gain the greatest benefit from this exercise, begin slowly so that it can be executed from start to finish without stumbling. When correct execution is mastered at a slow tempo, gradually increase the speed. Practicing with the metronome will keep the relationship between the duple and triple rhythms accurate.

For example:

A trill exercise, marked according to the counting table, would look like this:

1   2   3   4   1 + 2 + 3 + 4 +   1 ta ta 2 ta ta 3 ta ta 4 ta ta

1 ta + ta 2 ta + ta 3 ta + ta 4 ta + ta   1   +   2   +   3   +   4   +

1   +   2   +   3   +   4   +

This system for counting out loud works very well for everything except very slow movements in which 32d and 64th notes are used extensively, and sections with many subdivisions in compound time. In these situations it may be necessary to use eighth notes for the count of one beat instead of quarter notes.

Step 2: Write the counting in the score.

The following strategy for writing in the counting will ensure successful integration of an ornament *no matter how complex the score*:

1. First write in the main beats of each measure (1, 2, 3, etc.). Then write in the eighths ("and" or "+"). Follow that with the 16ths ("ta"). If there are triplets, write "ta-ta."

2. Write the counting *between* the staves. This ensures that the numbers are directly below (or above, in the case of the left hand) the notes to which they apply. (Write fingering indications above and below the staves to prevent confusion.) See the musical example below.

1 ta + ta 2 ta + ta 3 ta + ta   1 ta +   ta 2 ta + ta 3 ta + ta   1 ta +   ta 2 ta + ta 3 ta + ta

J. S. Bach. Polonaise in G Minor, *BWV Anh. 119, measures 1–3* [34]

---

[34] Palmer, *Bach: An Introduction*, 22.

3. Write 16th notes in *every* measure if they are used in *any* measure (as shown by the writing of "ta's" in the previous example). Even if there is only one 16th note in a piece, the counting of the entire piece should be subdivided into 16th notes. This prevents stumbling over 16th notes and ensures that each note is given its proper value.

Step 3: Measure all trills to master them.

To "measure" a trill means to specify the number of repercussions that are to be played in the time value of the main note.

For example:

The same example may also be realized as follows:

Trills can consist of two, three, or more repercussions, provided they fit into the time value of the main note. It is much easier to approach and depart from a trill when the number of repercussions is clearly specified and adhered to. (When the performer is comfortable with the execution of the trill and can integrate it into the rhythm of the passage, strict measuring of the trill may be relaxed. For greater expressivity it is permissible, for example, to begin the repercussions of a long trill slowly, gradually increase the speed and then decrease it at the end. It is also possible to begin a trill by lingering on the first note, thereby creating the leaning effect of an appoggiatura.)

MOZART'S TRILL EXERCISE

A helpful exercise for learning how to execute trills smoothly is Mozart's Trill Exercise, handed down to us by one of his most famous pupils, J. N. Hummel.[35]

Practice the entire exercise slowly at first, then gradually increase speed. Counting 1-ta-and-ta out loud while practicing will lead to even greater mastery and control.

Step 4: Use a metronome to ensure precise rhythm.

In the first step, a system for counting out loud was presented. In addition to counting out loud, practicing with a metronome was recommended to ensure precise rhythm. Humans are flexible; metronomes are not. Counting rhythms often seems accurate, but metronomes tell us the truth.

Step 5: Begin learning rhythmically complicated passages at a comfortable speed and gradually increase to performance tempo.

Learning to play a passage rhythmically accurately at a comfortable speed and gradually increasing the speed until the performance approaches the desired tempo has many advantages compared to trying to play a passage at performance tempo immediately. The advantages include:

- not introducing errors by trying to play a passage at too fast a speed too soon

- not reinforcing those errors

- ensuring accurate performance because the passage is always played at a manageable tempo

- being able to measure progress by the increase in the metronome setting at which the passage is played accurately

- increasing speed without sacrificing accuracy.

---

[35] Willard Palmer, Morton Manus and Amanda Vick Lethco, *Alfred's Basic Piano Library, Lesson Book, Level 5* (Van Nuys, CA: Alfred Publishing Co., Inc., 1983), 14.

Ornamentation: A Question & Answer Manual

A Teaching Strategy for Integrating a Fioritura Smoothly into a Performance

The key to smooth execution of a fioritura is to make sure that approximately equal numbers of additional notes are played against each accompaniment note. As defined in chapter 1, a fioritura is a series of additional notes played against a series of accompaniment notes, with the configuration of the accompaniment notes specified by the composer. More precisely, the accompaniment notes are described as consisting of *groups* of notes and the fioritura as consisting of *blocks* of notes.

There are no problems when the composer arranges the fioritura so that the number of additional notes is divided evenly by the number of accompaniment notes. Difficulties arise when there are more than one accompaniment note per group or when the number of additional notes does not divide evenly by the number of accompaniment note groups.

An effective strategy is to partition the additional notes into the same number of blocks as there are accompaniment note groups. The blocks should be of nearly equal length. Each block is then partitioned into sub-blocks by dividing the number of notes in the block by the number of accompaniment notes in the group. Finally, the first note of each fioritura sub-block is paired with its accompaniment note, and these notes are played simultaneously.

To illustrate, consider the following examples:

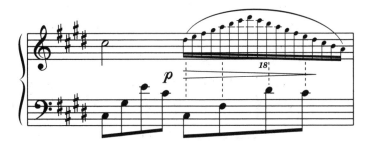

Frédéric Chopin. Nocturne in C-sharp Minor *(Posthumous), measure 58*

In this measure, the fioritura has 18 notes in beats 3 and 4, and the accompaniment has four single notes.

1. Because the number of additional notes (18) does not divide evenly by the number of accompaniment groups (4), we partition the accompaniment notes into two groups of two (4 ÷ 2 = 2) and simultaneously partition the additional notes into two blocks of nine (18 ÷ 2 = 9).

2. Each fioritura block is then partitioned into two sub-blocks. Because the number of notes in the block (9) doesn't divide evenly by the number of notes in the group (2), one sub-block will have four notes, the other five.

3. Then pencil in a line connecting the first note in each sub-block to the accompaniment note with which it will be played.

4. Play the passage to determine which group will have four notes and which will have five. The ear and hand will lead to the best decision.

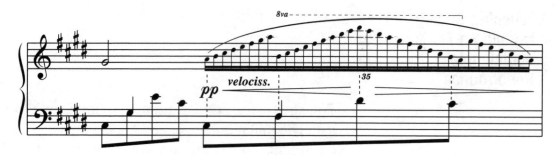

Frédéric Chopin. Nocturne in C-sharp Minor *(Posthumous), measure 59*

In this measure, the fioritura has 35 notes in beats 3 and 4, and the accompaniment has four single notes.

1. Because the number of additional notes (35) does not divide evenly by the number of accompaniment groups (4), we partition the accompaniment notes into two groups of two (4 ÷ 2 = 2) and simultaneously partition the additional notes into two blocks. The fioritura number does not divide evenly, so one block of 17 and one block of 18 fioritura notes is formed.

2. Each block is then partitioned into two sub-blocks. For the 18-note block, each sub-block has nine notes; for the 17-note block, one sub-block has nine notes and one has eight.

3. Then pencil in a line connecting the first note to each sub-block to the accompaniment note with which it will be played.

4. Play the passage to determine which group will have nine notes and which will have eight. The ear and hand will lead to the best decision.

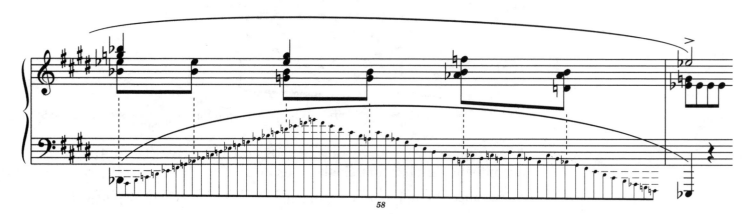

Frédéric Chopin. Etude in C-sharp Minor, *Op. 25, No. 7, measure 27*

In this measure, the fioritura has 58 notes in beat 4, and the accompaniment has three pairs of notes, forming three groups.

1. Because the number of fioritura notes (58) does not divide evenly by the number of accompaniment groups (3), (58 ÷ 3 = 19 + 1 remainder) partition the accompaniment notes into nearly equally blocks (19, 19 and 20).

2. Each block is then partitioned into two sub-blocks corresponding to the number of accompaniment notes per group (2). The number of notes in a 19-note block doesn't divide evenly, so use sub-blocks of 10 notes and then nine; for the 20-note block, the two sub-blocks have 10 notes each.

3. Then pencil in a line connecting the first note in each sub-block to the accompaniment note with which it will be played.

4. Play the passage to determine which group will have 10 notes and which will have nine. The ear and hand will lead to the best decision.

This system will help to ensure that performance is rhythmically accurate. Then the expressive possibilities of stretching and pushing the rhythms (tempo rubato) may be explored. If good taste is used, the wishes of all composers from the Baroque era to the present time will be fulfilled.

An Example

In J. S. Bach's "Adagio" from *Concerto No. 3 in D Minor for Oboe*, BWV 974 (item no. 3581, published by Alfred Publishing Company), the authors have realized all of the ornaments in accordance with the principles set forth in this book.

Summary

1. Use the procedure presented for correctly realizing an ornament.

2. Count out loud while practicing (see chart on page 51).

3. Write the counting in the score.

4. Measure all trills to master them.

5. Use the metronome to ensure precise rhythm.

6. Begin learning rhythmically complicated passages at a comfortable speed, and gradually increase to performance tempo.

7. Partition the fioritura notes into sub-blocks of nearly equal length, one sub-block for each accompaniment note, in order to ensure smooth execution of a fioritura.

Chapter 8
Adding Ornamentation to Baroque Music

To encourage performers to experiment and become comfortable with adding embellishments to Baroque music, Willard A. Palmer shows some ways that J. S. Bach's "March in D Major" from the *Notebook for Anna Magdalena* may be elaborated. The original text is reproduced,[36] followed by Palmer's elaborated version.

March in D Major
BWV Anh. 122

from the *Notebook for Anna Magdalena*

36 Palmer, *Bach: An Introduction*, 12–13.

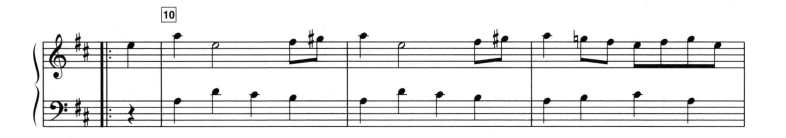

March in D Major

with optional varied repeats

SECTION A:

Varied repeat of SECTION A:

Varied repeat of SECTION B:

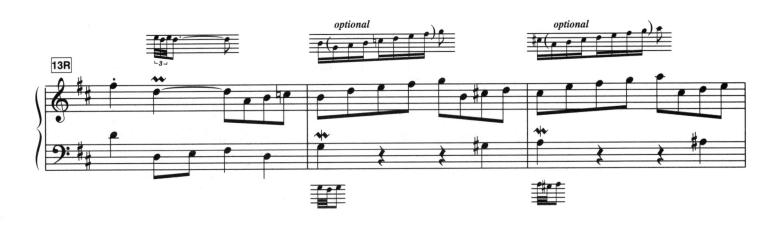

In addition to ornaments, it is possible to add:

- *passing tones* to melody notes that move by skip or leap[37]

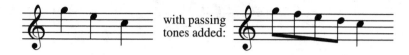

with passing tones added:

- *changing notes* that move in various patterns around or between the main notes of the melody.

with changing notes added:

Further suggestions on the possibilities of adding embellishments are offered in two of the tables provided by J. J. Quantz.[38]

J. J. Quantz, a court musician of Frederick the Great who played all of the Baroque instruments, left many tables of "added variations." The following tables contain selected excerpts from two of the original Quantz tables. Table 1 shows three notes moving upward by steps, and 17 different ways of adding free embellishments to them. The second measure shows the basic harmony that accompanies the motive to be embellished.

Table 1:

---

[37] Palmer and Halford, *The Baroque Era*, 8.
[38] Ibid.

Ornamentation: A Question & Answer Manual

Table 2 shows five notes moving downward by steps, and 13 suggested variations. The second measure shows the basic harmony that accompanies the motive to be embellished.

Table 2:

To use embellishments freely in performance, a performer needs to be familiar with many possibilities. Playing these two tables frequently will provide that familiarity. Then, using an embellishment becomes a matter of transposing it into the key of the piece. It is not necessary to play the same embellishment in the same passage each time; embellishments may be interchanged or even left out. Experimenting with adding the embellishments provided in the tables may spark other creative ideas, thus truly allowing free embellishment.

Bibliography

d'Anglebert, Jean-Henri. *Pièces de Clavecin,* 1689 (Pieces for Harpsichord). Quoted in Dannreuther, Edward, *Musical Ornamentation.* New York: E. F. Kalmus, n.d.

Bach, Carl Philipp Emanuel. *Essay on the True Art of Playing Keyboard Instruments.* Translated by William J. Mitchell. New York: W. W. Norton, 1949.

Clementi, Muzio. *Introduction to the Art of Playing on the Piano Forte.* London: Clementi, Banger, Hyde, Collard and Davis, 1801; reprint of first edition, second issue, New York: Da Capo Press, 1974.

Couperin, François. *L'Art de toucher le Clavecin* (The Art of Playing the Harpsichord). Edited and translated by Margery Halford. Van Nuys, CA: Alfred Publishing Co., Inc., 1974.

Dannreuther, Edward. *Musical Ornamentation.* New York: E. F. Kalmus, n.d.

Dolmetsch, Arnold. *The Interpretation of the Music of the XVII and XVIII Centuries, Revealed by Contemporary Evidence.* London: Novello, 1915.

Donington, Robert. *The Interpretation of Early Music.* Newly revised and enlarged version. New York: W. W. Norton, 1989.

Halford, Margery, ed. *Scarlatti: An Introduction to His Keyboard Works.* Van Nuys, CA: Alfred Publishing Co., Inc., 1974.

Hummel, Johann Nepomuk. *Aufführliche theoretisch-practische Anweisung zum Piano-Forte Spiel, vom ersten Elementar-Unterrichte an bis zur vollkomensten Ausbildung* (A Complete Theoretical and Practical Course of Instructions on the Art of Playing the Piano Forte, Commencing with the Simplest Elementary Principles and Including Every Information Requisite to the Most Finished Style of Performance). Vienna: 1828. Quoted in Dannreuther, Edward, *Musical Ornamentation.* New York: E. F. Kalmus, n.d.

Mozart, Leopold. *A Treatise on the Fundamental Principles of Violin Playing.* Translated by Editha Knocker. London: Oxford University Press, 1951.

Newman, William S., trans. "Emanuel Bach's Autobiography," *Musical Quarterly* 51 (Summer 1965): 366–72.

Palmer, Willard A., ed. *J. S. Bach: An Introduction to his Keyboard Music.* Van Nuys, CA: Alfred Publishing Co., Inc., 1973.

_____. *J. S. Bach: Inventions and Sinfonias.* Van Nuys, CA: Alfred Publishing Co., Inc., 1968.

_____. *J. S. Bach: The Well-Tempered Clavier, Volume 1.* Van Nuys, CA: Alfred Publishing Co., Inc., 1981.

_____. *W. A. Mozart: An Introduction to his Keyboard Music.* Van Nuys, CA: Alfred Publishing Co., Inc., 1974.

Palmer, Willard A., and Margery Halford, eds. *The Baroque Era: An Introduction to the Keyboard Music.* Van Nuys, CA: Alfred Publishing Co., Inc., 1976.

_____. *The Classical Era: An Introduction to the Keyboard Music.* Van Nuys, CA: Alfred Publishing Co., Inc., 1977.

_____. *The Romantic Era: An Introduction to the Piano Music.* Van Nuys, CA: Alfred Publishing Co., Inc., 1978.

Palmer, Willard A., and Amanda Vick Lethco, eds. *Introduction to the Masterworks for the Piano.* Van Nuys, CA: Alfred Publishing Co., Inc., 1976.

Palmer, Willard, Morton Manus and Amanda Vick Lethco. *Alfred's Basic Piano Library, Lesson Book, Level 5.* Van Nuys, CA: Alfred Publishing Co., Inc., 1983.

Quantz, Johann J. *Essay on a Method of Playing the Transverse Flute.* Translated by Edward R. Reilly. London: Faber and Faber, 1976.

Sadie, Stanley, ed. *The New Grove Dictionary of Music and Musicians.* London: Macmillan, 1989. S.v. "Ornaments" by Robert Donington.

Sonneck, Oscar George, ed. *Beethoven: Impressions by his Contemporaries.* New York: G. Schirmer, Inc., 1926.

Wolff, Konrad. *The Teachings of Artur Schnabel: A Guide to Interpretation.* London: Faber and Faber, 1972.